Sweeping Tsunamis

Louise and Richard Spilsbury

www.heinemann.co.uk/library
Visit our website to find out more information about **Heinemann Library** books.

To order:
 Phone 44 (0) 1865 888066
 Send a fax to 44 (0) 1865 314091
🖥 Visit the Heinemann Bookshop at www.heinemann.co.uk/library to browse our catalogue and order online.

First published in Great Britain by Heinemann Library, Halley Court, Jordan Hill, Oxford OX2 8EJ, part of Harcourt Education.
Heinemann is a registered trademark of Harcourt Education Ltd.

Editorial: Andrew Farrow and Dan Nunn
Design: David Poole and Paul Myerscough
Illustrations: Geoff Ward
Picture Research: Rebecca Sodergren and Debra Weatherley
Production: Edward Moore

Originated by Dot Gradations Limited
Printed in China by WKT Company Limited

ISBN 0 431 17868 2 (hardback)
09 08 07 06 05
10 9 8 7 6 5 4 3 2 1

ISBN 0 431 17869 0 (paperback)
09 08 07 06 05
10 9 8 7 6 5 4 3 2 1

British Library Cataloguing in Publication Data
Spilsbury, Richard, 1963 –
Sweeping tsunamis. – (Awesome forces of nature)
1. Tsunamis – Juvenile literature
I. Title II. Spilsbury, Louise
551.4'7024
A full catalogue record for this book is available from the British Library.

Acknowledgements
The publishers would like to thank the following for permission to reproduce photographs:

Associated Press p. **19**; Corbis pp. **7** (Charles O'Rear), **15** (Todd A. Gipstein), **22** (David Butow), **27** (Wolfgang Kaehler); p. **9** EPA/Mike Nelson; Getty Images pp. **4, 28**; Getty Images/AFP pp. **17** (John Russell), **20** (Jewel Samad); NOAA pp. **11**, (Pacific Tsunamis Museum), **26**; Oxford Scientific Films p. **13** (Mary Plage); Rex Features pp. **5, 12, 21**; Reuters p. **14** (Enny Nuraheni); Scanpix Nordfoto/EPA/AFP p. **18**; Science Photo Library pp. **23** (Carlos Munoz-Yague/LDG/EURELIOS), **25**; Te Papa Tongarewa Museum of New Zealand p. **24**.

Cover photograph reproduced with permission of AGE Fotostock/Imagestate. Unlike in this picture, tsunamis rarely break as they reach the shore.

Contents

*Any words appearing in the text in bold, **like this**, are explained in the Glossary.*

What is a tsunami?

A tsunami is a huge destructive ocean wave. It is nothing like an ordinary wave. As ocean waves move into shallow water, their narrow foaming tips curl over and 'break' (collapse). A tsunami hits land as a dark, fast-moving ledge of water that rarely breaks as it nears shore. Most tsunamis are barely noticeable in deep parts of oceans, but they get bigger as they approach land.

TSUNAMI FACTS

! The biggest tsunamis are the most destructive waves on the planet.

! The fastest tsunamis in the world can reach speeds of 800 kilometres per hour.

! Tsunamis have reached heights of 40 metres above the normal level of the sea.

Big tsunamis may move towards the land at hundreds of kilometres per hour. This photo, of a first tsunami wave, was taken by a tourist on the island of Penang, Malaysia, in December 2004.

Awesome force

Big tsunamis are like huge walls of water. They can be tens of metres tall and several kilometres wide, containing millions of tonnes of water. The water smacks hard onto land with the same force as a wall of concrete.

Anything in the way of a big tsunami – from people to giant ships or lorries – may be swept away, crushed or buried under water. Trees and telegraph poles are snapped like matchsticks. Homes, schools and lighthouses may collapse as if made of cardboard. Over the past 100 years, tsunamis have killed tens of thousands of people and caused millions of pounds' worth of damage around the world.

Harbour waves

'Tsunami' is a Japanese word that means 'harbour wave'. It was given this name because of the great devastation caused around the coastal harbours of Japan by many tsunamis.

The 2004 Indian Ocean tsunami caused flooding on Koh Racha Island, in Thailand. This shows one of the three large waves that destroyed a luxury hotel.

What causes a tsunami?

Tsunamis usually happen when giant chunks of land at the bottom of the ocean drop down as the result of an **earthquake**. Millions of tonnes of seawater move in to fill the gap. This causes a series of waves on the surface of the ocean – a bit like the ripples that spread out when you drop a stone into a pond or lake.

Earth movements

The outer layer of the Earth is made of solid rock. On mountain tops it can be bare, on deserts it may be covered with sand, and in oceans it is covered with seawater. Incredibly, this rock is always moving, although it does this very slowly. Deep inside the Earth it is so hot that the rock is melted into a sticky liquid. The cooler, lighter rock of the surface floats around on top of this liquid in enormous chunks called **plates**.

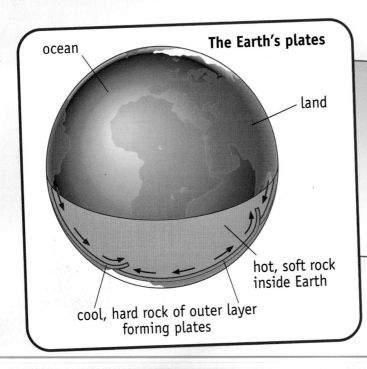

The Earth's plates

ocean

land

hot, soft rock inside Earth

cool, hard rock of outer layer forming plates

As the Earth's plates move, they push and slide against each other. Sometimes the plates stick and then one suddenly slips down, causing an earthquake.

Other causes of tsunamis

All tsunamis start when massive amounts of seawater are suddenly moved. Sometimes the **lava** in the Earth spurts out at gaps or thin spots in the plates. This is what we call a **volcano**. When underwater volcanoes explode, they destroy rocks around them and this can start tsunamis.

Tsunamis can also be started when large amounts of rock or ice on mountains suddenly break free and fall into water. Tsunamis would even happen if a large meteorite (a piece of rock from space) plunged into an ocean.

In 1883, the Krakatoa volcano in Indonesia erupted. The whole island collapsed and caused 35-metre high tsunamis that sped towards neighbouring islands, killing 36,000 people.

Deep beginnings

Tsunamis move outwards from the point where they start. Imagine you are on a plane flying over an ocean. If an earthquake struck hundreds of metres below on the **seafloor**, all you would see is crumpled water for an instant. The sea would then flatten again and a tsunami would speed away.

Tsunamis travel fastest in deep water. The **crest** of a tsunami in deep water may be only one metre tall. This crest is just the tip of a deep wave that reaches tens of metres into the water. As the wave moves towards shallower water, its bottom slows down as it touches the seafloor but the top pushes forward at speed. The water then bunches up and the tsunami is at its tallest as it reaches the coast.

Tsunamis can build to great heights as they get closer to land. Although they slow down, they can still hit coastlines at hundreds of kilometres per hour.

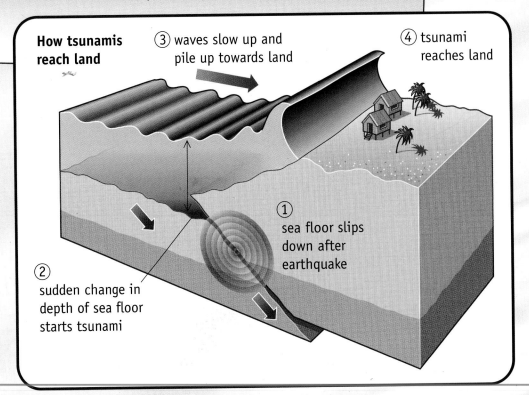

How tsunamis reach land

③ waves slow up and pile up towards land

④ tsunami reaches land

① sea floor slips down after earthquake

② sudden change in depth of sea floor starts tsunami

Enormous forces

Tsunamis shift immense quantities of water at such speed that they can travel over very long distances. In 1960, an earthquake off Chile in South America started a tsunami. The tsunami travelled 15,000 kilometres in 22 hours before hitting the coast of Japan. A big tsunami is barely slowed down when it flows over a small island, but it usually stops after it hits a **continent**. Some large tsunamis bounce back off continents and move back and forth over whole oceans, getting gradually weaker, over several days.

Tsunamis and tidal waves

Tsunamis are sometimes wrongly called tidal waves. Tidal waves are waves caused by tides. Tides are the regular rise and fall of the level of the oceans, caused by the pull of **gravity** of the Moon and the Sun. Especially high tides sometimes cause large tidal waves, but never tsunamis.

After the first tsunami waves, weaker waves continue to hit the mainland, adding to the damage. Here, the town of Hakkeduwa in Sri Lanka is being hit by the later waves of the 2004 Indian Ocean tsunami.

Where do tsunamis happen?

Most tsunamis happen in the Pacific Ocean. Some of the countries most at risk from tsunamis are Japan, the USA, Papua New Guinea and Chile, because they border the Pacific. Tsunamis happen here because a part of the Earth's outer surface, called the Pacific **plate**, lies underneath the Pacific Ocean. There are lots of **earthquakes** and **volcanoes** along the edges of this plate, where it meets other plates. This area is often called the 'ring of fire'.

Where else do they happen?

Tsunamis affect other coasts where earthquakes happen in the ocean. They have hit countries in the Indian Ocean, Canada, which is at the edge of the Atlantic Ocean, and countries in the Mediterranean Sea.

The countries around the edge of the Pacific Ocean are all at risk from tsunamis. But certain Pacific islands, such as Hawaii, are at particular risk because they are in the middle of the ring of fire. Tsunamis can approach from all sides!

The Ring of Fire

RUSSIA

Alaska (USA)

CANADA

San Francisco
USA
Los Angeles

Tokyo
JAPAN

Hawaii (USA)

PAPUA NEW GUINEA

PACIFIC OCEAN

INDONESIA

AUSTRALIA

CHILE

NEW ZEALAND

KEY
||| ring of fire

Shape of the land

Some parts of coasts are more affected by tsunamis than others. Towns and villages in greatest danger are those at **sea level** less than two kilometres from the sea. Even quite small tsunamis can travel a long way over flat land like this.

Tsunamis are also dangerous in curved bays or at the end of **fjords** (river valleys with steep sides). The waves get very high between their narrow sides. When tsunamis reach **headlands**, which are narrow strips of land sticking out to sea, they wrap around it. Then water floods onto land from both sides.

TSUNAMI FACTS

! The highest tsunami ever recorded happened in Lituya Bay in Alaska in 1958. A **landslide** fell into the narrow fjord, causing a wave over 500 metres high – that's nearly as tall as the CN tower in Canada!

Tsunamis can roll much further inland over a flat coastline like this, than they can over a steep or hilly shore.

What happens in a tsunami?

Tsunamis move very fast. If someone sees one approaching, then it is probably too late for them to get away from it! Sometimes, though, there are signs that a tsunami is on its way.

Many tsunami survivors describe how the **sea level** drops. Water is suddenly sucked away from the shore, uncovering sand, mud and reefs on the sea floor and leaving fish and boats stranded. The reason for this is that the water has moved to fill the space on the ocean floor created by an **earthquake**. Then the water returns in waves.

'I saw the entire bay suddenly drain of water with a quiet roar.' Mark Vanderkam, a survivor of the tsunami that hit Thailand in 2004

Before the first tsunami waves arrive, the sea is sucked back from the shore. This is what it looked like at Galle in Sri Lanka right before the 2004 tsunami hit.

Wave train

As the sea gurgles out from land, there is sometimes a very strong wind. This is air being pushed in front of the speeding tsunami. A big tsunami often comes in a series of waves called a wave train. The time between each wave **crest** may be minutes or even as long as an hour. Between each tsunami crest there is a **trough**, when water is again sucked out to sea. It seems like the water is being pulled by an enormous vacuum cleaner before it shoots back!

The first tsunami may not be the worst – the biggest, most dangerous waves in a wave train are often the third and eighth waves to arrive. After the tsunamis have struck, it may take days before normal ocean waves get back to their expected sizes.

The first tsunami wave to break may not cause the most damage. Other, more damaging waves, may arrive later.

Destruction

A big tsunami can destroy almost anything in its path. In an instant, whole areas of homes, farms and factories may be ruined. Many animals and people may be drowned under metres of water, or carried up to a kilometre inland. Cars, trains, boats, buses, shattered buildings and bridges are carried inland at high speed, like missiles. They may crush other things in their way.

The whole of a coastline may be altered by a tsunami. The seawater may flood large areas of low-lying land, ruining farmers' **crops**. Trees, other plants and soil are sometimes stripped from the land, and the sucking action of the wave train may shift whole beaches.

Tsunamis can cause horrific devastation. Whole cities were flattened as a result of the Indian Ocean tsunami in late December 2004. This was the city of Banda Aceh in Indonesia.

After the waves

When a tsunami is over, daily life does not return to normal for some time. Many people, such as fishermen with broken boats, cannot earn money because they cannot work. Children may not be able to go to school. There are many health hazards. Drinking water and **sewage** get mixed with seawater when pipes are snapped and **reservoirs** broken. People may then drink **polluted** water containing germs that will make them ill. Many are at risk of **electrocution** from damaged **powerlines**. Sometimes gas that leaks from broken pipes explodes.

When the seawater drains away, massive amounts of **debris** left on land have to be cleared up. Some debris comes from collapsed buildings or trees. Other debris is from the ocean – tsunamis pick up tonnes of sand, coral, rock and fish as they approach land.

After a tsunami, there is often a stench from piles of rotting fish dumped on land.

The Indian Ocean, 2004

On the morning of 26 December 2004 a huge earthquake shook the seabed off the Indonesian island of Sumatra. A tsunami sped away across the Indian Ocean, travelling at speeds of 480 kilometres an hour. The thousands of people who were working, playing and relaxing on the coasts of eight countries had no idea the tsunami was coming. Their only warning was when the sea suddenly pulled back hundreds of metres from the shore. The first wave caught most people unawares. Indonesia, Sri Lanka, Thailand and India were hit the hardest and about 250,000 people died.

'A great wave came rushing in to the shore, destroying everything and sweeping away everybody who was in the way. Everyone vanished in a second. The whole town was destroyed, along with people at the bus stand and vehicles on the road.'
Deepa, Sri Lankan survivor

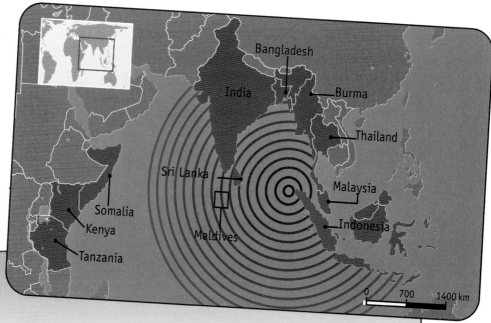

The circles on this map show how the earthquake that began near Indonesia caused a tsunami that travelled as far as the coast of East Africa.

Damage

Many people were injured and thousands of homes, hotels and businesses were destroyed. Countries as far away as the Maldives and Somalia were affected. The costs of aid, clearing up and rebuilding were in the region of US$6 billion. The rest of the world was shocked by the scale of the disaster and money flooded in to help victims and restore basic services.

After this disaster, scientists called for a tsunami early warning system around the Indian Ocean, like the one in the Pacific Ocean. Next time warning sirens could be sounded to give people a chance to escape to a safer place.

TSUNAMI FACTS

! The 2004 tsunami took fifteen minutes to reach Indonesia and seven hours to reach Somalia.

! Many victims drowned picking up fish flung on to the beach by the first waves.

People ran for their lives when the tsunami hit the shore of Koh Raya, Thailand, in 2004.

Who helps when tsunamis happen?

Many people help the victims of tsunamis. Scientists tell coast guards and government officials if there has been an **earthquake** that might start a tsunami. Then fire, police and ambulance services, and the navy are put on alert. Hospitals prepare to treat tsunami victims.

Authorities use radio and TV **broadcasts** to warn people that they may have to **evacuate**. They might also visit people where they live to tell them. If a tsunami is definitely on its way, sirens may be sounded so that people know they must evacuate to a safe place. Most people can travel on their own, but some young, old or sick people need help evacuating. The police and army usually help organize evacuations.

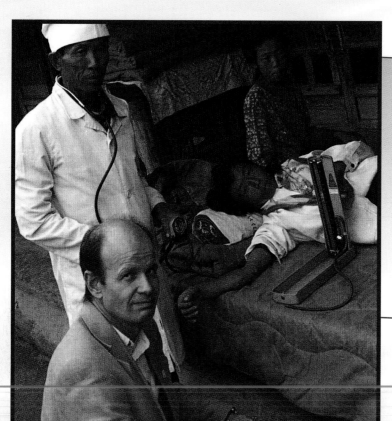

Local authorities and **charities** such as the Red Cross give **first aid** to injured people. They also collect together food and water supplies and organize shelter for evacuated people.

Emergency help

More help is needed if a tsunami happens unexpectedly, or if it affects more land than expected. Emergency services find and rescue people washed out to sea or trapped in dangerous places such as boats or unsafe buildings. Fire services put out fires of spilt oil or gas. **Paramedics** and doctors give first aid for injuries such as wounds and broken bones.

In some poorer countries, emergency services may not be able to cope with a tsunami disaster. They will ask for **aid** from other governments and international organizations and charities. Many of these groups may also help over a longer period, working with local people to rebuild homes and hospitals. In places where farms have been destroyed, they give seeds and **livestock** so people can feed themselves again. They also give new pipes and pumps to provide a safe water supply.

This rescue team has landed in a helicopter. They have sniffer dogs to help them find people who may be trapped in collapsed buildings.

What to do when a tsunami happens

- People who live or work on the coast should move two to three kilometres inland or to higher ground.
- People on a boat on deep sea should stay there and not return to land. The height of waves is lower further out to sea, over deep water.
- People should keep a radio or telephone nearby to listen out for further warnings and messages.
- People should never return to a tsunami-hit area until they are told the waves have stopped coming.
- People should keep away from buildings left standing after a tsunami, because they might collapse.

People on boats near coasts should head out to sea if they hear a tsunami warning. Boats near the coast will be tossed and smashed onto the land like toys, like this boat in Banda Ache, Indonesia, in 2004.

Japan, 1993

On 12 July 1993 an **earthquake** struck 20 kilometres off the island of Okushiri. The Japanese authorities gave a tsunami warning on radio and TV within 5 minutes, so many people were able to **evacuate** to higher ground. However, waves 5 to 30 metres high had already struck Aonae, a fishing village on Okushiri's southern **headland**. Over 200 were killed by the waves.

The Japan Maritime Safety Agency used helicopters, boats and divers to find missing people. Heavy cranes and bulldozers were used to clear **debris** that had filled the harbour.

The sports hall of Aonae Middle School became a temporary shelter for hundreds of people whose homes were destroyed. Their new homes were built further away from the sea, so any future tsunamis would affect them less.

This photograph of Aonae was taken the day after the tsunami in 1993.

Aonae

SEA OF JAPAN

JAPAN

PACIFIC OCEAN

Can tsunamis be predicted?

Scientists around the world work together to predict tsunamis. They use machines called **seismographs** to record when and where **earthquakes** strike and how strong they are. If a big earthquake happens under or near an ocean, the scientists warn neighbouring countries that it may cause a tsunami. However, not every earthquake starts a tsunami, so scientists have developed ways of detecting and tracking tsunamis.

Detecting waves

There is a network of special research stations around the Pacific Ocean that measure the heights of tides. Scientists use these stations to notice sudden changes in water level that happen before a tsunami. Scientists from Japan and the USA have laid cables on the ocean floor, near their coasts. Special boxes along the cables sense when a deep tsunami wave passes over them. The boxes send this information via **satellites** to scientists onshore, so that they know a tsunami is on its way.

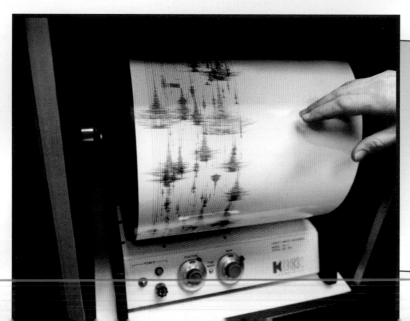

The marks on this paper show earth movements recorded by a seismograph. The more the ground shakes, the bigger an earthquake is.

Looking into the future

Many countries use powerful computers to help them **simulate** how tsunamis will affect their coasts. To do this, they prepare special electronic maps of coastal places, showing where people live, and what the land around is like – for example if it is flat or hilly. They also put in information about previous tsunamis, such as how far they travel on flat land and up steeper slopes. They then simulate different sizes and speeds of tsunamis hitting these places.

Simulations like this are vital to work out the best places to **evacuate** people. Local authorities can then tell people the quickest escape routes if a tsunami approaches. Simulations also show people where the safest places to build are.

These are computer simulations of tsunamis hitting land. They give people a good idea of what might happen if a tsunami were to hit their coast.

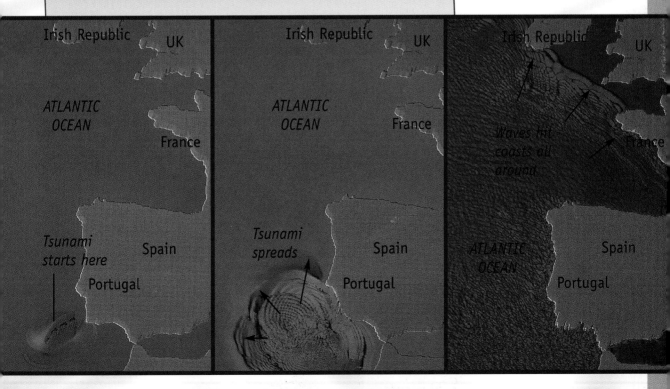

Irish Republic   UK

ATLANTIC OCEAN

France

Tsunami starts here   Spain

Portugal

Irish Republic   UK

ATLANTIC OCEAN   France

Tsunami spreads   Spain

Portugal

Irish Republic   UK

Waves hit coasts all around   France

ATLANTIC OCEAN   Spain

Portugal

Can people prepare for tsunamis?

People who live in places threatened by tsunamis must understand the danger they are in. They can then prepare in various ways, from the way they build their houses to knowing how to **evacuate**.

Building for tsunamis

The damage caused by tsunamis can be reduced if buildings are made stronger. For example, most of the repair costs after the Aonae tsunami (see page 21) were spent mending damaged harbour walls. Since then new, taller, strengthened sea walls have been built around parts of Japan. In Hawaii, many office and hotel buildings are now designed on stilts – the ground floor is open parking space with rooms above. The water should then pass through the open space and not damage the building structure.

This museum in New Zealand is shaped so that waves can move around it. It is also built on special rubber feet so waves can move it 75 cm without damaging it.

Evacuation plans

It is vital for people to know the best way of getting themselves, their family, pets and farm animals to a safe place. All family members should know how to contact each other or where to meet if they are not all in the same place. They should also know things about where they live and understand evacuation warnings. People should always take evacuation warnings seriously. They should also look out for tsunami signs such as sudden changes in sea level.

A tsunami survival kit

If people have to evacuate, they should take the following:

- a **first-aid** kit and any essential medicines
- enough food and water for at least three days
- a torch and radio with extra batteries
- warm clothing, blankets or sleeping bags
- money and important papers such as passports and their driver's licence.

US states bordering the Pacific Ocean have put up tsunami signs like this, which show people the way they should go if they hear a tsunami warning on the radio or television.

Papua New Guinea, 1998

In July 1998, an **earthquake** started a giant underwater **landslide** that caused an immense tsunami. It was dusk when three huge waves swept over Arop and other villages around Sissano lagoon in northern Papua New Guinea.

Earthquakes are common in Papua New Guinea because it is near the join between two of the Earth's **plates**. However, most of the local people did not know about tsunamis. A rumble was heard out at sea and many people moved closer to see the sea drawing back and then rising above the horizon. Those who could, ran for their lives. The first wave flooded the land and broke up the villagers' flimsy wooden houses. The second wave, which was ten metres high, swept everything away in front of it. Two whole villages were completely destroyed. Thousands of people were injured or killed, many by being thrown against trees or being hit by floating **debris**. Many of the victims were children.

Before

After

These pictures show a village centre before and after the tsunami of 1998. Whole buildings were wiped out by the tsunami's awesome power.

Sissano

PAPUA NEW GUINEA

PACIFIC OCEAN

Future safety

After the disaster, Australian emergency services and **charities** such as Oxfam worked with the government of Papua New Guinea to look after survivors. They provided **aid** and helped them rebuild their lives. They also showed local people what to do if another tsunami happened.

Charity workers and the government of Papua New Guinea produced posters, leaflets, special TV programmes and videos about tsunamis. They took these to all the coastal villages and told local people what to do if a tsunami happens. In November 2000 another, smaller, tsunami struck, but amazingly no-one was killed. Most people had remembered their lessons. They had climbed to high ground as soon as the earth began to shake and the **sea level** changed.

In Papua New Guinea, children are now taught all about tsunamis at school. Teachers explain that Papua New Guinea has been hit by many earthquakes and tsunamis, and tell the children what to do if a tsunami happens.

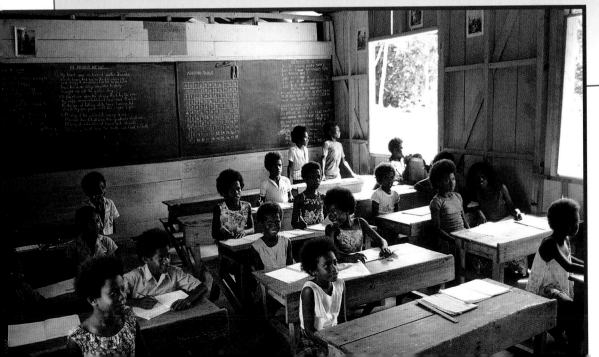

Can tsunamis be prevented?

Tsunamis are natural events that have happened throughout the history of the Earth. Just as we cannot stop **earthquakes** or **volcanoes**, we cannot prevent tsunamis. There has been at least one tsunami a year in the Pacific Ocean since 1800, and there will be more in future. Big tsunamis that affect the coasts of many countries happen around once every seven to ten years.

Changing world

As the population of the world grows, coastal towns and cities get bigger. This means that each tsunami may affect more people. Some US states have areas of sand and gravel on their coast. These were dropped there by big tsunamis in the past when few people lived there. If a big tsunami happened now, millions of people on the US Pacific coast might be affected.

The key to dealing with tsunamis in future is to be prepared by learning what they are and what to do if one happens.

Tsunami timeline

1908, Calabria, Italy
After an **earthquake**, a 15-metre high tsunami killed almost 100,000 people.

1933, Sanriku, Japan
An earthquake created a tsunami that killed 3000 people, broke 9000 buildings, and overturned 8000 boats. The waves were felt as far away as Iquique, Chile.

1957, Alaska
This Pacific-wide tsunami damaged coasts in Alaska, British Columbia, Washington, Oregon, California and the Hawaiian Islands. Waves were as high as 23 metres.

1960, Chile
One of the most destructive Pacific-wide tsunamis, this tsunami created waves up to 25 metres high. In Chile up to 5700 people died and about 2,000,000 were left homeless. The tsunami also killed 61 people in Hawaii.

1979, San Juan Island, Colombia
250 people were drowned when a tsunami destroyed all the houses on the island.

1993, Japan
A tsunami with waves of up to 31 metres high hit the Japanese island of Hokkaido. 239 people were killed, but early warning systems prevented the impact of the tsunami being greater.

1998, Papua New Guinea
A tsunami cause by an earthquake off the northern coast of Papua New Guinea, killed 2182 people, injured 1000 and left 10,000 homeless.

2004, South-East Asia
An earthquake off the Indonesian island of Sumatra created a tsunami that caused the death of about 250,000 people. Indonesia, Thailand, India and Sri Lanka were worst hit but the waves travelled as far as Somalia in East Africa.

Glossary

aid help given as money, medicine, food or other essential items

broadcast programme (on radio or TV) that gives information to many people

charity organization that gives out aid and makes people aware of disasters

continent seven large land masses on earth – Asia, Africa, North America, South America, Europe, Australia and Antarctica

crest highest point

crop plant grown by people for food or other uses

debris broken pieces of buildings, trees, rocks, etc.

earthquake shaking of the ground caused by large movements inside the Earth

electrocution when someone is injured by electricity

evacuate move away from danger until it is safe to return

first aid first medical help given to injured people

fjord narrow strip of sea between high cliffs

gravity force which attracts objects together and which holds us on the ground

headland strip of land sticking out into the sea

landslide when a large piece of land suddenly slides down a slope

lava melted rock from inside the Earth that comes out of a volcano

livestock animals kept by people to eat or to sell

paramedic medical worker who travels to where an accident has happened to help people

plate sheet of rock that forms part of the surface of the Earth

polluted when air, soil or water is poisoned or dirtied

powerlines cables that carry electricity

reservoir large natural or man-made lake used to collect and store water

satellite object made by humans and put into space. Satellites do jobs such as sending out TV signals or taking photographs.

sea level normal level of the sea's surface and land that is at the same level

seafloor solid bottom of a sea or ocean

seismograph machine that records the force and direction of an earthquake

sewage waste matter from toilets and drains

simulate to show accurately how something would happen

trough a wave's trough is its lowest level

volcano hole in the Earth's surface through which lava, hot gases, smoke and ash escape

Find out more

Books

DK Eyewitness Guides: Discover the Power of Volcanoes and Earthquakes – from Hot Spots and Black Smokers to Devastating Tremors and Tsunamis, Susanna van Rose (Dorling Kindersley, 1992)

Floods and Tidal Waves, Terry Jennings (Belitha Press, 1999)

Websites

www.howstuffworks.com – this website contains a detailed explanation of how earthquakes work.

www.fema.gov/kids/tsunami.htm – this website gives facts about tsunami dangers, including what to do and how to prepare.

www.tsunami.org – the website of the Pacific Tsunami Museum, which has photos and stories of tsunamis in the past.

Index

Titles in the *Awesome Forces of Nature* series include:

Hardback   0 431 17828 3

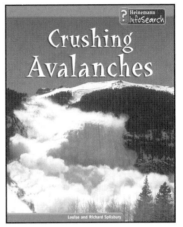

Hardback   0 431 17831 3

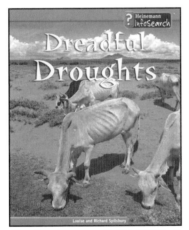

Hardback   0 431 17829 1

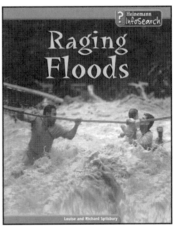

Hardback   0 431 17830 5

Hardback   0 431 17832 1

Find out about the other titles in this series on our website www.heinemann.co.uk/library